Part II

Compiled by Joan Frey Boytim

Laura Ward, *pianist*

To access companion recorded accompaniments online, visit:
www.halleonard.com/mylibrary

2673-7683-9912-3984

ISBN 978-1-4234-1216-8

G. SCHIRMER, *Inc.*

DISTRIBUTED BY

HAL•LEONARD®

7777 W. BLUEMOUND RD. P.O. BOX 13819 MILWAUKEE, WI 53213

www.schirmer.com
www.halleonard.com

Contact Us:
Hal Leonard
7777 West Bluemound Road
Milwaukee, WI 53213
Email: info@halleonard.com

In Europe contact:
Hal Leonard Europe Limited
Distribution Centre, Newmarket Road
Bury St Edmunds, Suffolk, IP33 3YB
Email: info@halleonardeurope.com

In Australia contact:
Hal Leonard Australia Pty. Ltd.
4 Lentara Court
Cheltenham, Victoria, 3192 Australia
Email: info@halleonard.com.au

PREFACE

The success of the books in the series *Easy Songs for Beginning Singers* indicates that there is a need for more preparatory literature of this type for middle school and high school singers in early stages of traditional vocal study. Teachers have commented to me that in some colleges these books are even used with very inexperienced freshmen, or with beginning adult singers.

The volumes of *Easy Songs for Beginning Singers—Part II* are at the same level as the original books. They can be used alone or in conjunction with the first set. Based on a teacher's choice of songs, there is no reason that a student could not easily start in *Part II*. Both volumes of *Easy Songs for Beginning Singers* lead very nicely into *The First Book of Solos* series (original set, *Part II*, or *Part III*).

There are 18-20 songs per volume in *Easy Songs—Part II*. A number of the selections have been out of print and will be unfamiliar to some teachers. All the songs chosen are very melodic and should pose no major musical or vocal problems for beginners of all types.

The compilation theory behind these volumes remains basically the same as in the original set. All songs are in English, some in translation, to keep the music easier to learn and comprehend. We have used songs with moderate ranges and tessituras to facilitate the building of technique. The wide variety of music includes folksongs, early show songs, operetta, parlor songs from c. 1900, as well as very easy art songs.

The art song composers include Schubert, Schumann, Franz, Arensky, Rimsky-Korsakov, Grieg, Quilter, Ireland, Head, Hopkinson, Beach and Dougherty. Operetta and vintage popular composers include Kalman, Romberg, Herbert, Berlin and Meyer. Care has been taken to provide the male voices with masculine texts. Some "old chestnuts" which young people may have never experienced include "Glow Worm," "Trees," "The Bells of St. Mary's," "Somewhere a Voice is Calling," and "Because."

My wish is that this set of books provides more options for the novice singer of any age, and helps all of my fellow teachers with the ongoing aim to lead more students into the joys of classical singing. Incidentally, these volumes may also be another source of relaxed and fun material for experienced singers.

Joan Frey Boytim
May, 2006

CONTENTS

The price of this publication includes access to companion recorded piano accompaniments online, for download or streaming, using the unique code found on the title page. Visit **www.halleonard.com/mylibrary** and enter the access code.

AUTUMN

Monica Hillier

C. Alison-Crompton

FOR ME AND MY GAL

Edgar Leslie and
E. Ray Goetz

George W. Meyer
(1884-1959)

COLORADO TRAIL

American Folksong
Arranged by Celius Dougherty
(1902-1986)

to Dr. Livia Frege
FAREWELL
(Gute Nacht)

Joseph von Eichendorff
English version by Arthur Westbrook

Robert Franz
(1815-1892)

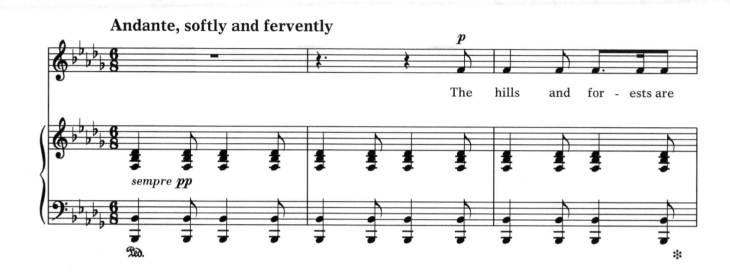

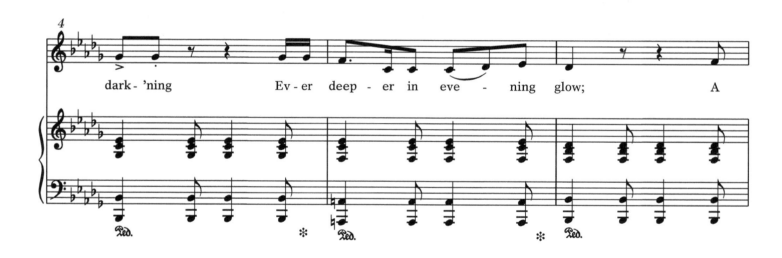

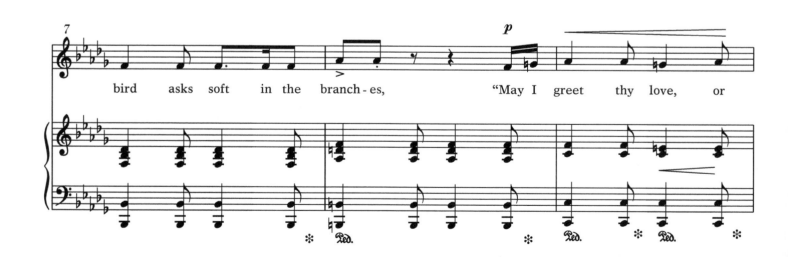

GIVE MY REGARDS TO BROADWAY

text by the composer

George M. Cohan
(1878-1942)

Give my re-gards to Broad - way. Re-mem-ber me to Her - ald Square. Tell all the gang at For - ty - Sec-ond Street that I will soon be

there. _____ Whis-per of how I'm yearn - ing to min-gle with the old - time throng. _____

Give my re - gards to old Broad - way and say that I'll be

there, 'ere long.   long. _____

GYPSY LOVE SONG
(Slumber On, My Little Gypsy Sweetheart)

Harry B. Smith

Victor Herbert
(1859-1924)

1. The birds of the for-est are call-ing for thee, _____ And the shades and the glades ____ are lone - ly; _____ Sum-mer is there with her blos - soms fair, _____ And you ____ are ab - sent

2. The fawn that you tamed has a look in its eyes _____ That doth say: "We are too ____ long part - ed;" ____ Songs that are trolled by our com - rades old, _____ Are not now, as they were, ____ light-

THE HAPPY LOVER

Old English Melody

Arranged by
Henry Lane Wilson
(1871-1915)

ing, be - guil - ing, Re - pents

her dis - dain.

Trans - port - ed with pleas - ure, I gaze on my

HE'D HAVE TO GET UNDER –
GET OUT AND GET UNDER
(To Fix Up His Automobile)

Grant Clarke and
Edgar Leslie

Maurice Abrahams
(1883-1931)

Johnny O' Connor bought an automobile,___

Millionaire Wilson said to Johnny one day,___

17
He took his sweet - heart for a ride one Sun - day, John - ny was togged _
Your lit - tle sweet - heart don't ap - pre - ci - ate you, I have a daugh -

22
_ up in his best Sun - day clothes, _ She nes - tled close _ to his
- ter who is hun - gry for love, _ She likes to ride _ by the

27
side. _ Things went just dan - dy 'till he
way, _ John - ny had vi - sions of a

31
got down the road, _ Then some - thing hap - pened to the
mil - lion in gold, _ He took her rid - ing in his

old ma - chine - ry, That en - gine got ___ his goat, Off went his hat _
lit - tle au - to, But ev' - ry time ___ that he Went to say "mar -

_ and coat, Ev' - ry - thing need - ed re - pairs. _____ He'd
- ry me," 'Twas the old sto - ry a - gain. _____

have to get un - der, get out and get un - der To fix his

lit - tle ma - chine, _____ He was just dy - ing to

* This repeat is optional.

hug and kiss ____ And then the darned old en - gine

it would miss ____ And then he'd have to get un - der, get

out and get un - der, And fix up his au - to - mo -

1. bile. _____

2. He'd bile. _____

D.S.

to Maggie Teyte

HER ROSE

Jeanie Gallup Mottet

Charles Whitney Coombs
(1859-1940)

Rose - bud, you touched her, You breathed _____ with her breath And her

sighs; Fair rose, you kissed her, You

to Walter Creighton

HEY, HO, THE WIND AND THE RAIN

William Shakespeare

Roger Quilter
(1877-1953)

IT WAS A LOVER AND HIS LASS

William Shakespeare

Gerard Barton
(1861-?)

KASHMIRI SONG

Laurence Hope

Amy Woodforde-Finden
(1860-1919)

Moderato assai con molto sentimento

Pale hands I loved be - side the Sha - li - mar,*_____ Where are you now? Who lies be -

neath your spell? Whom do you lead on Rap-ture's road-way, far,_____

*Gardens

wav - ing me fare - well.

Pale hands I loved be - side the Sha - li - mar,

Where are you now? Where are you

now?

THE MAN WHO BROKE THE BANK
AT MONTE CARLO

text by the composer

Fred Gilbert

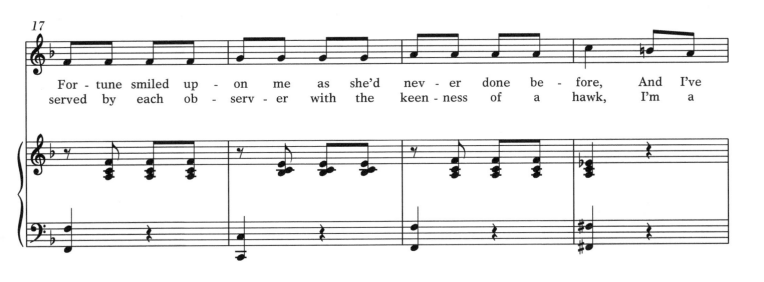

For - tune smiled up - on me as she'd nev - er done be - fore, And I've
served by each ob - serv - er with the keen - ness of a hawk, I'm a

now such lots of mon - ey I'm a gent._____ Yes, I've
mass of mon - ey, lin - en, silk, and starch_____ I'm a

now such lots of mon - ey, I'm a gent._____ As I walk a - long the
mass of mon - ey, lin - en, silk, and starch._____

Bois Boo-long, With an in-de-pen-dent air, ____ You can hear the girls de-clare ____ "He must

be a Mil-lion-aire;" ____ You can hear them sigh, And wish to die, You can see them wink the

oth-er eye At the man who broke the Bank at Mon-te Car-lo. ____

THE SAILOR'S LIFE

Old English Melody

Arranged by
Henry Lane Wilson
(1871-1915)

1. A sail - or's life's the life I trow, He works now late now ear - ly; Now up, now down, now to __ and fro: What __ then? he takes it
2. If howl - ing winds and roar - ing seas Give proof of com - ing dan - ger, We view the storm, but rest __ at ease, For __ fear's to Jack a

laugh a lit-tle, And work a lit-tle, and play a lit-tle, And fid-dle a lit-tle, and

foot it a lit-tle, As brave-ly as __ we can. can.

3. But think not that our

life is hard, Though storms at sea ill-treat us; For com - ing home's a

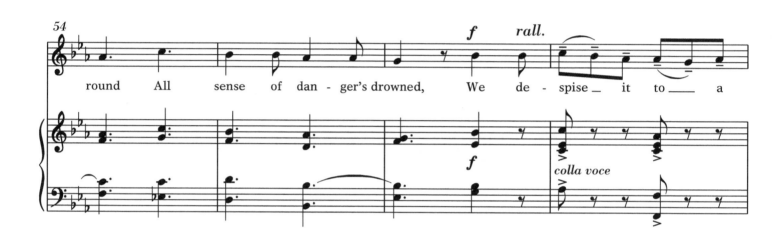

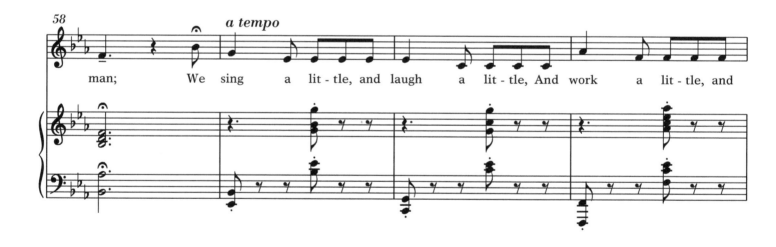

RED RIVER VALLEY

19th Century American Folksong
Arranged by Celius Dougherty
(1902-1986)

THE ROAD TO PARADISE

from
Maytime

Rida Johnson Young

Sigmund Romberg
(1887-1951)

Valse lento e rubato

No hand to clasp in mine,

No guid - ing star!

Ah, Love, Lead me where you are,

In your lov - ing eyes, There is my Par - a - dise.

SOFT DEWS FROM HEAVEN FALLING
(Kein Hälmlein wächst auf Erden)

Albert Emil Brachvogel

Wilhelm Friedemann Bach
(1710-1784)

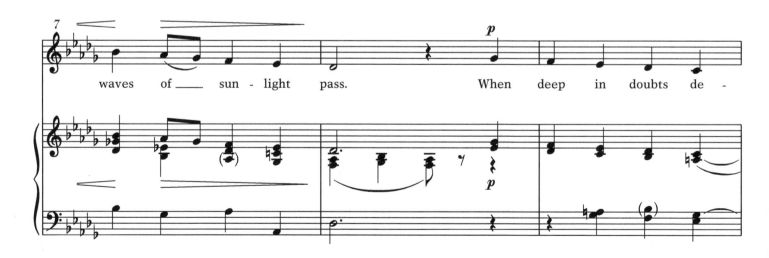

THE WATER IS WIDE

English Folksong
Arranged by Christopher Ruck

SYLVIA

Clinton Scollard

Oley Speaks
(1874-1948)

Andantino espressivo

Syl - via's hair is like the night, Touched with glanc - ing

star - ry beams; Such a face as drifts through dreams,

This is Syl - via to the sight. And the touch of

cantando